C000100922

SEEKING SERENITY

A Selection of Books by White Eagle

SEEKING SERENITY

WHITE EAGLE

*FINDING FREEDOM
FROM FEAR*

THE WHITE EAGLE PUBLISHING TRUST
NEW LANDS · LISS · HAMPSHIRE · ENGLAND

First published September 2007

© Copyright,
The White Eagle Publishing Trust, 2007

British Library Cataloguing-in-Publication Data
A catalogue record for this book is available from the
British Library

ISBN 978-0-85487-184-1

Set in 11.5 on 15 point Sabon
Printed and bound in Great Britain
by Cambridge University Press

CONTENTS

v

PREFACE

THIS BOOK, which was given through Grace Cooke, is appropriately entitled SEEKING SERENITY and contains much loving teaching from the spirit side of life to reassure the reader that all is well in the earthly life: that there are no mistakes and everything is in the care of a higher power. It is also a book about brotherhood, for White Eagle says that it is only by understanding what this concept means that humanity will really establish peace on earth so that that serenity may become widespread. Brotherhood is surely the religion of the Aquarian age—when there are no priestly hierarchies and no valid claims to private truth; when instead all realize their own contact with the Source or the Light within.

A further part of White Eagle's reassurance to us is that there is on the other side of life, where he himself dwells, a Brotherhood of Light or Brotherhood of the Star, who watch our progress and look after us. Our lives may be directed by the Lords of Karma, but there is an infinite care that comes to us from those who have progressed beyond our limited state and yet know the pain that may sometimes be involved in being human.

White Eagle was not content to let brotherhood be an ideal 'out there', but he has actually established, within the White Eagle Lodge, a brotherhood of servers upon the earth, with the conviction that if brotherhood could be established among the few, this model can influence the many. His teaching is collected and presented by that ongoing brotherhood, so that the changing selection by his editors over the years is also an indication that his teaching is a living one. SEEKING SERENITY is a book for now, even though one of the earliest phrase in this compilation, 'the secret of strength lies in the quiet mind' goes back to a teaching of 1936. He himself is forever intimately connected with the endeavour that bears his name; those that prepare the much-loved books of his teaching do so with his gentle voice echoing in their ears and the twinkle of his eyes before them.

INTRODUCTION

A MEDITATION

IN THE SPIRIT world is a beautiful garden, and everything that grows in it is an expression of the spirit of God. The flowers and trees, their colouring and perfume, the song of the birds and the play of the fountains, the layout of the garden itself: all are manifestations of the highest and purest Godlike thought. Angels help to create this garden. In the centre of the garden is a lake of crystal water reflecting the sky and the flowers and trees and the reflection makes the garden even lovelier. As the garden is reflected in the still waters of the lake, so is truth reflected in the human heart. But to reflect truth the heart must be tranquil, serene and still.

The spirit, the heart, or the mind of the heart, like the still pool at the centre of the garden, reflects pure truth from the mind of God. You can look into the pool, the mind of the heart, and see the law of cause and effect at work. You can see the reason for all that happens and the perfection of God's plan for the ultimate good and progress of humankind.

Standing by this lake and watching the reflection of

goodness and beauty, you may see your own reflection too; you see yourself as you are, in comparison with the beauty and glory of God and the manifestation of God's truth.

If men and women would cease from mental conflict, if they would enter the garden and learn to be still by the lake of truth, brotherhood would rapidly be established. Wars would cease, and that which is manifesting in heaven, in the garden of God, would manifest too on earth.

May the roses bloom in your garden, my brethren.

CHAPTER ONE

A PATH TO PEACE

*Be confident in the love and the wisdom of God;
darkness will not touch you if you are radiating
light.* Light is love and purity and all the qualities
of the Christ spirit. May the divine will sleeping
within you rise and direct your life.*

WE would lead you to the peace of the heavenly
life. Without this inner peace of the heavenly
life, you live in a state of stress and anxiety and fear.
The Brotherhood of the Star, who are so close to
your spirit always, work to dispel all the fears and
anxieties to which you on earth are subject. When
you are in trouble you become tense, and because of
the tension whatever you are suffering from is more
painful and the suffering increases. When there is
conflict in the mind there is no peace in the soul, but

---

*This is a keynote of another of White Eagle's books, THE BOOK
OF STAR LIGHT (1999).

when the spirit controls the mind and the nervous system, then peace and tranquillity rule. The love, the light in the heart, is pure spirit; and human life must be guided by the spirit. Once you can relax and relinquish your problems to God, all conflict ceases and health, wholeness and holiness return.

The experiences of your life are to help you to grow in consciousness of your real life, of your spirit, of your real self. You are part of the Great White Spirit, and as soon as you know this not only with your mind but with your innermost feelings—with your heart and your soul and your mind—you will feel safe and at peace: at peace with your circumstances, at peace every day of your life.

These are not merely fine words; what you can feel is the simple truth of the life of Christ in you. You may be human, but you are also divine, even as Christ was. It is for you on earth to allow the golden light to manifest through you. We come among you to help you at all times to respond to the power of love which flows from the heart of the Father–Mother God, and which, in degree, flows from the heart of every soul who is in tune with that great Source of life. This is eternal life: life that is infinite, life in which no soul can ever grow weary because it is life that is continually renewed. Therefore the soul can go on and on and on, never wearying, always refreshed, always recreating itself. God will give you strength to remain constant and true. Do not be tempted to look on the negative side. What you do not understand, leave aside; but never fail to trust God's love.

Keep on Keeping on

We come to you to help you. Just a thought from you—a prayer, a hope—and we know and are with you. We ask you to see the power of the eternal Spirit working throughout your life. See the unfoldment of the spirit taking place all around you. Think in terms of the smoothness of the power of God at work in your life, in your health, in your affairs. Do your best within your capacity and see this beautiful power of love, love of a father for his children, working through your affairs. All things are working together for good.

We know the sorrows and the difficulties of the material life. The path you lead is not easy, we know; and because the Brothers who have passed onward into the light understand the sorrows, the disappointments and the hardships of mortal life they come back with a great longing to help, to give you knowledge of your own inward powers, to tell you of those beautiful states of life which await you in due time. They will want to tell you how worthwhile your efforts will prove, to say that no effort is ever wasted, although you do not see results. Keep on keeping on your path. We promise you that it is leading to heaven,

13

to a life so full of bliss and peace as to be quite beyond your imagination.

We know how hard it is to pursue the darkened path. You have to walk in darkness, to accept the conditions in which you find yourselves, trusting in the love of the Great White Spirit, trusting that the eternal arms are always around you and that your earthly experiences come for a wise purpose. We know you will say, 'This is all very well, White Eagle. We believe what you tell us. But how is your promise going to affect our present-day difficulties and problems?'.

Some of you have been through sorrow and separation; some have been anxious on account of your loved ones, and some are confused in mind and heavy in heart. All these things we know and we are with each one of you individually. We are pointing the way towards your goal; and when your vision is fixed upon that goal you will acquire a different mental and emotional attitude to your companions and the problems of everyday life. For what we have to tell you is the way to overcome these problems. You and we know that the eternal Light is the great solvent of all problems—but humankind does not make the effort to rise in thought and aspiration to the life which is light and joy and tranquillity because contacting this Light requires the subduing of the lower nature, which is of the earth.

We come back to offer you truth; to love you and to inspire you to look up towards God. All your little difficulties will then pass away. All are transient, and no obstacle is insurmountable. Do your best. Do not worry about tomorrow, but be calm and patient. Your Father–Mother in heaven knows your need.

You must trust God. When you realize this, you find deep peace. If your motive is good, you are good. God is taking great care of you, and at the right time whatever you hope for will come to you. On earth you see all the difficulties and problems and you judge other people. You judge life because it is not to your liking; but when you realize that all you can see has a purpose and is helping humanity to evolve, to develop understanding, then you will know that all is well.

Happiness is your Goal

It is good for you to expect happiness, to endeavour to create and share happiness. It is accepted by many thinkers that humanity is born to suffering. We prefer to look upon the other side of the coin! We are convinced that God created human beings to be happy.

Happiness is your goal, my brethren; not misery, not suffering, but joy, and happiness must necessarily be shared. You cannot be happy to yourself alone; to be wholly happy, you must be sharing heaven. And so the purpose of all the teaching that comes to us from the White Brotherhood above is to point the way to happiness. If we pray to our Father–Mother God for the strength to do so, we shall attain happiness; and in doing so we shall be able to help many souls to the same state.

You can always safely leave your problems and difficulties to divine Law, if you yourself live in harmony with that Law and surrender yourself to it, accepting your karma as part of your spiritual unfoldment. *Not a sparrow shall fall on the ground without your Father, but the very hairs of your head are all numbered.* But so often you forget, and you think that God and the spirit people have forgotten you and do not understand your suffering. They understand only too well, my children, the fears and the pain in your heart, but you have to learn that there is always a beautiful outcome. You cannot assess suffering. You see so little of the whole picture. We are trying to help you to understand the purpose of pain and the corresponding joy that is the outcome. Think of the cross not as a symbol of suffering, but of renunciation, surrender: a giving up of the self-will. With this renunciation there comes such a calm peaceful joy, a realization that all is well. The lessons you can learn from your earthly experiences are so valuable because they are helping you to grow spiritually, and in your knowledge and understanding of life, spiritual life as well as physical. These opportunities are offering a deep richness of soul, the power to enjoy life on the earth plane, the power to receive spiritual joy and ecstasy—a happiness beyond the power of words to describe.

So, dear brethren, do not turn resentfully from your karma, or from the difficulties that confront you from time to time. Face them with courage, and ask to be shown the mystery that they contain. We would assure you that your earthly problems, if accepted and worked out rightly, will bring to you in due time happiness and fulfilment. We know these things are true.

We know also that you dear earthly brethren have to learn to have faith and trust in the Great White Spirit, who holds the plan of your life. We can truly say to you that good cometh, light cometh out of darkness. Light comes with the rising of the Sun, the sunlight in your soul. What may seem sorrow to you at first will in due course be revealed as a great opportunity—because through your disappointment, through your sorrow, the seed of the spiritual harvest will have been sown.

All is Well

God never hurries. Be patient; control your haste. All is well. As you are patient, you will learn too of the infinite tenderness and the wisdom and the love of God, and this knowledge will bring the assurance that all is well. If only we could impress upon you all that there is a most certain and definite path of eternal progress before you, and that all works together for good, you would find that deep peace in life for which you long! You cannot waste time if you are attuned to the eternal life, for then all works together in harmony for you. Give your hearts in simple, childlike faith to your Creator, and try to feel that the angels are very close to you.

To be aware of God is to possess faith. Faith is beyond all factual knowledge. Faith is a voice in the heart which whispers, 'I am here, my child; I am by your side; I supply every need. My ways are wisdom and love. Whatever life brings is by my love and my will, because I know your need and my love holds no limits'. This great love is enfolding you, and so long as you are willing to be enfolded in this heart of love it will hold you and give you sweetness and comfort and strength; it will give you inspiration to walk bravely on your allotted path. It will give you companionship, it will give you love and joy indescribable. It will in time reveal to you the whole glory of God's life.

In simple ways the Lord comes: quietly, silently. The angels are singing, 'Peace on earth and good will'. You are passing through the mists into the sunlight, dear brother, dear sister.

CHAPTER TWO

TRUST IN GOD

If you are able to put your confidence in God, it means that you are absolutely at peace; nothing is wrong. If you have confidence in God you are untouched by anything the world can do.

The Way of Confidence

IF YOU HAVE confidence in spiritual law, it will never, never fail you. Whatever you are called upon to go through, look up to the heavenly light, to the Divine spirit. You will never regret your faith, your confidence in the power of God not only to bring you through the wilderness but to bless you with understanding of the purpose of your sorrow or tribulation.

Have no fear. Place your whole confidence in God, your Father–Mother. Look into the future with confidence in God and do not see the worst but *always the best.* God knows your need, and the need of each one of you varies. Follow the law of brotherhood and all your needs will be supplied. Your problems will be dissolved; they will fade away as the morning mists fade when the sun grows strong. This is exactly what happens in human life. When you are directed to look towards the light and to open yourselves to the light—to be still and enter the power and the love of God—the light floods your consciousness and all heartbreak and anxiety disappears.

In simple language, we would say that your Father–Mother in heaven knows what is good for every one of you. You must trust God. This is such a simple message to give you! We do not use profound and intricate language to convey truth to you. We give you what you need, each one of you.

Have you lost one who is nearest and dearest to you, and are you searching in vain while the heavens seem to be as brass? Rise through earnest prayer, direct to Christ who understands your sorrow and your need; the heavens will open and the comforter come into your heart. Your eyes will open, and you will see your loved one and be reunited.

Are you sick or faced with the illness of one you love? Then rise in spirit to meet the glory of the Golden One, Christ, in the heavens, and all sickness and pain will be healed, for He is the great healer.... Turn to the Golden One; be patient and rest in faith—indeed, in full consciousness of His wisdom. You have no need to be anxious or fearful if you accept the love and wisdom of your Creator who loves you and guides you step by step.

Nothing is as important as you think it is. The most important thing in your life is your quiet relationship with your Creator, your Father–Mother God—all wisdom and all love. Do try to keep very quiet and peaceful and do what you can at the physical level quietly and without strain. God will help you. More strength will come, and if things do go a little criss-cross, let them go, be above it all! You will not get the tangle out of your wool by pulling at it.

Just leave it. Give your confidence to God and the tangles will all fall out. This is the wise way to live. Relax, keep calm, do your best, and leave the rest to God.

Surrender your Problems to God

Surrender means a deep certainty in the soul that all is held in God's hand, and all is working for good. Then the divine life takes possession and works miracles. A miracle, it is said, is something apparently outside the working of natural law. Truly, miracles are the natural outworking of divine law in the physical state. Those who do not understand divine law say, 'Lo, a miracle has happened!'. But miracles start, my brothers and sisters, in your own soul. If you can take hold of that

21

deep inner truth which tells you that Christ's kingdom is in you, and that you live in Christ's kingdom of the Star, of brotherhood and love, it must manifest in your life, in your surroundings. This is the natural law: as above so below; as below so above!

If you could only surrender yourself to God's law and understand that what is happening to you is all part of a perfect outworking of this law, you could then be at peace. When you think about spiritual truth and are confronted with so many human problems, you feel confused and quite unable to answer all the questions. They seem so diverse and contradictory that you say, 'I cannot understand. It is beyond me'. Yet, as you advance step by step on your path, you will find that your questions will all be answered and everything will fall into place. You will see the cause, the reason for all. Above all, you will see that the answer to every human problem lies in the simple word 'love', which is harmony, which makes all crooked places straight.

Therefore withdraw. Withdraw yourself from whatever human problem is yours at this very moment. Drop it: in other words, surrender it to the Divine Spirit. Have confidence in the Source of your being, the Great Light. Your problem will then no longer trouble you, for you will know deep within yourself that God will answer your need and all will be well. The answer to all your problems lies in surrender. This is a spiritual state to which the soul has to attain. The one who has entered into the heavenly consciousness, surrenders his–her life and actions into the keeping of the Most High. When the soul has truly learned to surrender all, then the power will work.

Look up to the Light

We see a beautiful shining light that is beyond the clouds, and so we bring to you this message of hope....

Peace be with you. All will be well. *All will be well.* Have no fear, brethren; you may rest quietly. Give your trust, that is all. Trust and have courage. The tests you are called upon to undergo have their bright side and the cloud has not just a silver lining but even a golden one. Oh, we do assure you that this is true! We see it so clearly for you all. It is a wonderful thing to be able to give yourselves in trust, and this is a realization that comes with brotherhood. We are all in the service of each other, of the brotherhood of all life, and surely this is joy and happiness? *All care will cease when the level of spiritual consciousness of brotherhood has been achieved.* The light within you, the inner voice, will tell you truly your duty; then do that duty, and look into the face of your Master with confidence.

We want you to realize that the light that you worship is part of your own soul, and that light shines in you and beautifies all earthy things for you. It is the beauty that you see on earth, the love that makes you happy, the power which comes to you when you seek God's blessing. The glory of that light is the divine fire within. If you will call upon this when you are weary, you will feel divine strength flowing through you, and all anxiety will fade away. Your vision will be upon the blazing Star and you will be in conscious contact with your higher self, your divine self, your eternal, age-old self. This will direct your actions and bring into your life all the blessings of the heavenly life. You will then be untouched by the little things that presently have power to disturb you.

Look up! Keep the vision of the Star, trust the power of the Star. If your heart is centred upon the Christ love with all your soul and with all your mind, you will indeed love your neighbour as yourself. You will be helping, so that brotherhood will become a reality on earth. On earth you are only aware of separation from each other: death, or distance, or perhaps lack of sympathy or misunderstanding will separate you. But when you come within the harmony of the Great White Brotherhood you are no longer separated from your loved ones, nor are you separated from the great masters or from the very Christ, the great light, the supreme light and love.

CHAPTER THREE

THE DIVINE PLAN

Whoever you are, wherever you are, you are guarded and guided along life's pathway. There is a divine plan for your life, and for humanity, and the wise teachers come very quietly and gently to try and impress this spiritual truth upon the human mind.

A Plan for Humankind

WE CAN see a glorious future for humankind when the injustices have been righted and men and women have learned the way of wisdom. We see the natural and beautiful coming together of all nations, united in one vast brotherhood; a time coming when human beings will understand their responsibility towards all the kingdoms of life! Be assured also that in world affairs right will conquer and justice will balance apparent wrongs. There will come an expansion of consciousness and humanity will look up beyond the astral planes to that celestial world where Christ and the angels and all the shining company of heaven dwell.

Do you know how the world is progressing? You may think that disaster lies ahead for some countries or people—but oh! if only you could see with a clear vision, you would see how great is the power of the Light in your brethren!

You think your world is in chaos; but we know that with the help of the many groups at the present time who are discovering the reality of life and who are praying for peace and goodwill, gradually, step by step (as if walking up a ladder, from earth to heaven), humanity is being raised. Humanity is doing a lot of talking and quarrelling, but it is learning, and it is gradually rising above those things of a material nature that are the enemies of humankind. You are gradually escaping from them, you are gradually overcoming your enemies, because you yourself are beginning to see light, truth. In very ordinary language, you are seeing common sense: which means the sense of rightness and harmony. We have said to you before that if you will transfer your thoughts from physical matter to spiritual life you will solve your problems. This is a truth. You cannot appreciate it at present; nevertheless, practise what we say. Do not think about physical conditions or problems of the earth.

Many are distressed about conditions on the earth plane; many are overwhelmed with fear, hoping for the best but fearing the worst. But we would tell you that we are happy about the evolution of the human race on earth. As we look upon the earthly conditions and all the complexities, we see a most wonderful development in humanity and in human life on the earth plane. You become disappointed by the disputes and misunderstandings between people and by the conflict between the races; but we see, beyond your mortal vision, a *wonderful* growth going on. We see rays being projected to the earth in love from this vast Brotherhood above—not only from evolved earthly souls but also from the Brotherhoods of other planets. You talk about love on your earth, but you have little understanding of the power and beauty of love as it is known on the higher planes. This love is always at work: this light, this tenderness, this understanding one for another and this outpouring of love and light to the earth.

It comes down to this: that every brother and sister, every single unit of life has an immense opportunity. If the light is generated and sent forth, you are acting to assist your companions respond to and absorb the light that is being sent to them. We have to remind you that you are being given a most glorious opportunity in your own individual lives in preparation for this New Age we are now entering. In the New Age there will be a complete removal of the heavy dark veil of prejudice and cruelty and selfishness that has hung across the human vision for many centuries. Because

27

this New Age is such a wonderful era in the history of the earth, we ask you neither to doubt, nor to fear or condemn. We see a great harvest, a golden harvest. But we need humanity to let go, take their hands off and allow the wisdom and the love of the Great White Spirit to take control!

It will come; and you are the servants, the agents for this work. You are not alone. There are many wise ones watching, inspiring, guiding. Do not think you are carrying responsibility for the right living, right action and right thinking of others. The only responsibility you are carrying is for yourselves.

We are sad sometimes when we see that you are sad—when we see you worried and confused and perplexed—and we long to bring you an assurance that will bring peace to your troubled hearts. If you would grow in spirit, you must become responsive to the shining company watching over you and helping you in your daily life. God knows the need of every soul on earth, for all are God's children. Try to understand that you are very dear to your Creator and that all that is happening now, both to you personally and in the world, is happening for a purpose, and is the outworking of a cosmic law. Out of pain and suffering and sorrow will come a beautiful unfoldment, as a flower in bud gradually unfolds in the warmth and the light of the Sun. Each one of you is like that flower, gradually unfolding.

Rise into the Light

Every life is cared for in its smallest detail. We can hear you say, 'But White Eagle, what about all the suffering and the tragedies that we see: where is the love in a God who allows these things to happen?' We are not unmindful of the tragedies enacted on earth, but we would like to explain to you that you can only see one aspect of what has happened, when you would consider it tragedy. What maybe you see as tragedy (when viewed with clear vision, and when the whole picture of the life can be seen) may be a beautiful happening, bringing immeasurable blessing to the soul. You will find it difficult to accept this, but we do want you to hold fast to belief in the law of love that governs all human beings, and to remember the limitations of your vision. For what may appear to you as tragedy will later on, with clear vision, be revealed to you too as a remarkable outworking of the Divine Law of love.

We would help you to rise above the problems of the earth plane into the light of the Sun, to be at peace within. As this purifying light and power flows into your heart you will be able to see with clearer vision the outworking of a plan that is so wise and so good, for all humanity: something not easy to see with the little mind of everyday life. But as you open your hearts to receive this blessing from the heart of the

29

Sun it will help you to see good, to see the outworking of a beautiful plan, in spite of the difficulties which are so apparent at the earthly level.

Remember, brethren, that all is working together for the great day of illumination of the whole of humanity!—for the great Brotherhood which is to be. You know, if you could see with your pure spiritual vision, you would see into the hearts of all people, and you would find, beneath all the rubble and the rubbish, a great sweetness every time. If you will cultivate this true vision, if you will learn to see truly from your heart, and if you will look deep enough, you will see goodness everywhere, in all peoples. Moreover, as you receive that blessing into your heart, it will flow through you, through the oneness you feel with all humankind. The light in you will flow to others, to all the world, to bless, to heal and to help stimulate that same beauty in every heart.

We in the world of light are asking you all to respond to this call. As you give you will receive, and as you receive so you will give.

The new world is shining behind the veil. Do not doubt; do not fear. Live continually in the company of the shining ones, your guides, your companions of the spirit. Do not be misled by commonsense and reason. They have their place and they give you balance, but do not be blindfolded by them. Look beyond, to the true life.

A Plan for your Life

Your life is working to a plan. Nothing can go wrong. You have no need to worry about decisions ... whether to do this, that or the other. Your decisions will be made for you when the time comes, but you must be awakened to the spirit, quickened in spirit, so that you will instantly respond to the gentle guidance of the presence within you. We would reassure every one of you that if you will truly follow the light within your heart, all *will* be well.

Just relax, and don't try to make things go the way you think they should go. Cultivate joy and laughter in your heart, and know this beyond all: that there is a very wise and loving plan for you. Don't set your heart on the way *you* want things to go, but centre your whole aspiration upon the light, and the realization of the power of the light in your own heart.

For we tell you, all things work together for good; there is a divine law pervading all life. Good comes out of ignorance and darkness. There is a plan, a wise plan for the spiritual growth of humankind. If you are anxious about the future, we would reassure you that all will be well and that there is a wise purpose in frustration and in suffering. *Every* soul seems to go through suffering, but if you can see it in the right perspective you will see that suffering is a rebirth.

Through limitation and suffering—the narrow path—the soul merges into the divine life and light just as the insect in the chrysalis stage emerges into a beautiful winged creature.

Life is governed by law; humans have to abide by the law of karma. Karma is a merciful law and ultimately it brings to every soul indescribable happiness. Hold fast to the truth of the spiritual life. Whatever your present karma, it is good. It is an opportunity given to you by divine law to grow in spirit and in happiness.

Each one of you is striving to reach your goal of the soul perfected, which will bring divine love and joy into your heart, and will bring you health. You find it difficult to accept that the sickness, loneliness or tribulation you have to deal with is your own soul's wish. But it is so. When you make a so-called mistake, it is a certain step forward that you have to take so that you may learn wisdom. It will bring you in the end to perfect love. Never blame other people for your troubles. Neither blame yourself. Instead, always look within and seek the divine love within your heart; then you will see the reason for the conditions that limit you, and you will see the work you have to do *within yourself*. You can only rise by making the effort to put aside all that troubles you and reaching up to the heaven world.

It is useless to kick against the circumstances of earthly life, for so long as you kick against them, you will surely have them obstructing your pathway.

Be happy, be at peace, be patient. Your work is in the plan. Every episode in your life is according to the plan of the Great Architect of the Universe. The plan will unfold when you yourself have learned a certain amount of wisdom, when you have been prepared, perhaps through extreme difficulties in your physical life. You have your work to do, and your troubles and frustrations are all testings and preparation—polishing you, making you a more receptive instrument for the power of the spirit. Think ill of no-one, for no-one is your enemy; all are your teachers. Once you can really accept and believe this you will be so much happier.

Do not think that we are unaware of the disappointments, the hardships and the fears that possess you. We in spirit know that you have tests. We know that the physical body is not always as fit and perfect as it could be. We know that the material conditions of your life can be a little tiresome. As we draw close to the physical plane, we are aware of how you feel the burdens of life. We would comfort those who are sad, those who are puzzled and perplexed. How can we best convey to you the love and the wisdom of the Eternal Spirit? It is foolish to fret; your problems always come right in the end. Nothing can hurt you, so why not walk with your hand in that of your guide, knowing that all is working out according to the plan? All things work together for good.

The Lesson of Patience

If you put a seed or a bulb in the ground, it won't be hurried. It will take its time to grow and eventually bloom. This is how spiritual power works. Your difficulty on earth is that you want things to hurry up. You want things to happen all at once, but spiritual power often works slowly. Do not live with the feeling that you must get over the ground as quickly as possible to reach a certain point. Just live every moment, every hour, every day tranquilly, taking the hours as they come and doing one thing at a time. Go forward each day with the spirit of brotherhood living in your heart. Keep on keeping on, although the hill seems insurmountable when you have to turn a corner and you cannot see the summit. Keep on persevering with your climb, knowing that the summit of that mountain is in the light of the sun, and that in due time all humankind will reach the summit.

Remember, one of the great lessons the pupil of the Master has to learn is that of patience: patience when you are confronted with material difficulties, patience to know that all will work out for good. You think this means waiting and waiting and waiting—endlessly. Indeed, we can hear some of you thinking, 'But we are patient, White Eagle. We *have* been waiting patiently'. The whole of life has to be composed of continuous patience, because right up to the very time

34

of your release from your physical body you will be learning this lesson. So bear patiently your difficulties and problems. If we can all keep on keeping on, thankfully and trustfully, along the appointed path, we shall be blessed with achievement, completion, happiness, such as the world cannot give, and peace such as the world cannot take away.

CHAPTER FOUR

YOU ARE NOT ALONE

Whatever problem you now face, beloved friend, face it in the light of Christ. Look into the face of the Master—the gentle, wise Elder Brother— and strive daily to live in thought, in company with the Master. And you will find that conditions will be made clear for you, the path before you will be straightened out.

Hand in Hand with Angels

BELOVED brethren, we bring all love from the world of spirit. Never think of the spirit world as removed from you. It is all around and within you, and will always guide you into the path of light.

We bring dear love to you all, and the assurance that you are not alone, that whoever and whatever you are, you are loved and helped. As you love others and as you help yourselves, so the help of angels comes to you, raising you up until your lives glow with joy and all becomes light. Never forget the angel by your side. Hold the hand of love and true humility in your work. Angel servers are always close. All they need is the co-operation of human love.

Remember this. They are great rays of power and strength, enfolding and protecting. From them emanate the God-forces. They mingle with those who have been incarnated in a human body. They work hand in hand with men and women. You can develop your awareness and your fitness to be a clear and true channel of those Angelic forces by communing with God each day, even if only for a short time. Just send your thanks to your Creator, and in the consciousness behind your active human brain dwell in the knowledge that the Angels are with you, the heavenly Hosts.

Strive to be simply good—simply kind and pure in thought, speech and action. Thank God for your life and all its blessings; for the beauties of the sunrise and sunsets, the beauties of the clouds and the skies. Enjoy the gentle rain without resentment at getting wet. Turn your face to the raindrops and thank God that Brother Water comes to give you life. Brother Air comes to give you life. For in all these elements are the angels, and when man understands this he becomes at one with the angels, he works hand in hand with the angels.

If you will be steadfast on the path to which your

feet have been guided—by brethren before you on that path—you will find the treasure of life, a never-ending stream of help and healing and happiness. We, your brothers and guides, are on the road by your side. Not one of you stands alone. You have only to ask in simple trust, and you shall receive; whatever your need, it shall be supplied. Each one of you has your own guide by your side, one who never leaves you. Your guide knows your innermost need and will comfort you and lead you into green pastures and beside still waters.

Some of you are faced with problems that seem to be insurmountable, and you may think that we in spirit know nothing of your own human needs and your difficulties. You do not realize how close we are, or that sometimes when you are out of your body, in your sleep, you come to us and confide your weakness, your worry, your sorrow. Your brethren over here understand and are waiting to help you. Do you know that many of these friends are around you now, acting as silent helpers, silent watchers, ever on the lookout for opportunities to serve and to help, to guide and to inspire you?

We who come from the inner world are well aware of the practical details of human life. You may think that being spirit we are quite remote from the activities and the pains and the fears and the sufferings of our brothers and sisters on earth, but here you would be very much mistaken. The Brotherhood of the

White Light is closely concerned with the evolution, happiness and wellbeing of all humanity. We have passed through many incarnations and have the means of recalling these human experiences when necessary. Therefore we can feel with you; we can understand your frustrations, your limitations and your anxieties and fears. We can understand physical pain and spiritual suffering. We are part of you; we are one of you; we are with all of you.

We Understand your Difficulties

We who have left behind us the bondage of earthly bodies understand the difficulties that confront our brothers and sisters in the physical life. You know the saying that 'the stones that cut the pupil's feet have first wounded the Master'? He has walked the selfsame path, and his feet have been cut also. We are so attuned to you, our brethren, that we absorb your feelings.

We do not speak in loud language of the things of the spirit. It is better not to shout from the hilltops, and so we just keep quietly on, you with us, and we with you. We are not unmindful of your grief, your anxieties, your disappointments. We share all these with you; but we can see beyond your vision, and the way we help you is by coming back from the spirit life to bring you hope and light. This we shall always do.

We know that every grumble, every depressing, fearful thought, can weave greyness and darkness into your spirit—which should be a radiant thing. You may wonder why sometimes you find it practically impossible to realize the presence of spiritual beings; and at others you feel so sure of the presence of your guide. Why is it that on certain days you feel blank and heavy? At another time you feel as if on a mountaintop, with clean bright air about you. You get distinct impressions from the spirit world; you feel so sure of your guide, and that everything is going to be all right. When they arise, the density and heaviness you experience are there because you are literally in a psychic fog—compared to the higher, spiritual sunlight you otherwise find. At such periods, cling with all your strength to the consciousness that the sun is there behind the mists: your helpers are still closely with you.

We know the sorrows of human existence because we have ourselves endured them. We know the heartaches, the disappointments of human life, its fears and doubts and terrors. We know also that behind the whole of human endeavour there is hope and light, kindled out of humanity's persistent thoughts of kindliness and goodwill. While we are here with you on earth we participate in your life, your thoughts, your sorrows—but we do not take them with us when we rise into the spirit realms. Instead, we bring happiness and love down to you.

You are not shut away from this glorious Brotherhood that we describe to you, or only insofar as you shut yourself away. You can close around you a barrier of despair and darkness and fear, and then you separate yourself from this Brotherhood, for the Brotherhood will never intrude upon your wish for isolation. But if you open your heart and say 'come' they come, so joyously, and will never fail to do so. We see, not the outer shell, but the beloved spirit, our true brother and sister, within the shell; it is because we can see this that we love you and do not see the mists, which are but the physical coverings.

Find Good in the Silence

This we advise you to do: seek in the silence to discover the beautiful jewel in your brethren. Love one another and see good in all men and women, deep within—see the jewel within the lotus. This will help you to keep your contact with the Brotherhood in the world of spirit. By this we do not mean only the exalted beings, but all those kindly, sincere, loving friends who are yours on the spirit planes of life.

So we of the Brotherhood come to lift you into the world of light and to help you to live, in thought, in our world of spirit. We are able to draw close to you at all times. We want you to realize this and call to us and speak to us on the inner planes. We will never fail to answer you, but you need first a greater faith and trust, and to disentangle yourselves from the doubts and fears of earth life. You *want* to believe, but you are not always strong enough. So we urge you to be true in your friendship and your love for these silent helpers. If the light of the Star shines from your heart, you open the way for shining brothers and sisters from the world of spirit to draw close and lead you through the doorway into the realms of light and truth. You are all like young plants with roots in the dark earth, and are struggling to send green shoots above the earth, and some flowers and blossoms. This is the purpose of everyday life, but it does need effort: effort from the spirit within you.

We want you to come up as often as you can into this sphere of harmony and truth, so that you become immersed in it—just as a sponge, immersed, becomes full of water. You will become full of the light and harmony of those higher spheres, and then the darkness will have no power over you.

The brothers in the spirit world can and will help you to solve every difficulty; for when you surrender yourselves and your life into the wise and loving keeping of your Father–Mother God, you break down the barrier that material thought has created, and the help you need flows to you. So, when you are perplexed and fearful, will you think of your brethren of the Lodge above, who, through the instrument of the golden Star, pour streams of golden light into the soul to awaken the Christ in you? Surrender, yield yourselves up to the golden light, and let it pour through every fibre of your being. Let it dissolve every disappointment and difficulty. Each time your eyes are opened to the right way of life, each time you are able to touch the secret inner life, the light expands in your heart and soul. Then life takes on a new aspect. You see with eyes both spiritual and physical a lovelier vista, a more profound beauty than you have seen before—and your heart will sing with praise and thanksgiving to your Creator.

Everyone is Tested, but not beyond his or her Strength

Do not think that we are unaware of the disappointments, the hardships and the fears that possess you. We in spirit know that you have tests. You are never alone.

Your need is understood, but every one of you, whoever you are, has to undergo tests. This is the secret you must try to understand. Every brother and sister is faced with many tests. You know, there is an old saying, 'God strengthens the back to bear the burden', and it is true. Each man and woman is tested, maybe to the very limit—but your strength rises to meet what is demanded of it, and your guide rejoices to see you strive earnestly. The tests can be uncomfortable, and make you unhappy; but they can also bring you lasting strength. They can bring you an increase of spiritual power and love, and so can fill you with indescribable happiness and joy.

Some of you pray earnestly for your problems to be removed. You long for the light and for wonderful spiritual ecstasy, but it is only by going through these outer things that your eyes are opened. You cannot taste and see until you have passed through this process and become able to absorb and comprehend the beauty of the heavenly life.

There may be some of you too who are heavy with sorrow because of the sufferings of those you love. It is very hard to have to remain still, to be unable to do anything. Whenever you witness suffering of the body or of the mind that you are unable to heal, try to remember that the sufferer is working through a condition of life which will eventually lead his or her soul into the light. Hold your beloved friend or dear one in that light, that hope. Hold them in the light of courage, which will help their soul to make good.

The Ordeal that is Growth

We assure you that you are on a path of ever-unfolding light and beauty and happiness. Do not look with dismay upon the petty irritations of your earthly life, or question why these things come. If you come up against a certain experience you would do anything to escape from or alter, and if the lesson proves hard to bear, then endeavour only to go through with a patient and steady spirit, knowing that it is perhaps karma that has to be endured. Whatever is placed before you in the work of tests, go calmly through and all will be well. Every time you are tested and stand up to your test with strength, you advance a step further on the path.

We would call these soul-tests minor initiations, sometimes major ones. Initiation means an expansion of knowledge. In your daily occupation you will be beset with tests. You can listen to words, but until you have passed a soul-test you know only with your mind, and not with your whole being; you have not acquired the true knowledge. You should be joyful, my dear ones, even in the face of difficulties, knowing that these difficulties mean that you have arrived at the point where you can clear away your karma. Sorrow, trouble, loss: they are not cruelly inflicted upon you by an avenging God. They are the working out of divine law, and an opportunity for you to take the next step forward on your path.

When you are confused and in doubt and are fearful of the result of your actions, remember that your soul is in your physical body to gain experience. There really *are* no burdens except those you yourselves pack up and put on your backs. God is all love, and does not inflict suffering on anyone. You create your own suffering and you pick up your own little burden and you strap it on your back. We know this, and that is why we would not wish to, why we cannot, dare not, interfere with your experience.

There is nothing to fear. You may not be able yet to see the way ahead—but know that at the right time, when you are ready, the way will be shown to you. You have nothing to be afraid of because all your needs are supplied and all is well. The test, dear ones, is that of the Christ Spirit. You cannot fail.

After you have come through a special ordeal you will say, 'I gained something. I felt something beautiful from it'. Remember this. However difficult, that experience will be worthwhile. We speak to you from the realms of spirit, and we speak truth: wisdom is attained only through experience, and experience is sometimes painful. You must experience, possibly through pain or fear or apparently making a mistake, for through experience you become attuned to the centre of the Christ Star and receive into your soul an increase of light—a deeper wisdom, a greater strength, and heavenly peace.

The fruits of suffering are wisdom, love and power—the power of the inner spirit, the power of love. You cannot attain wisdom suddenly. Only pray earnestly for the wise heart, the pure heart, the gentle loving heart, and you will be filled with happiness and joy. We would like you all to feel this inexhaustible flow of spiritual healing, spiritual power to evolve all earthly things in a most perfect form. May this blessing be yours!

CHAPTER FIVE

THE POWER WITHIN

You must live creating beauty in your mind. That which you think today, you will yourself become tomorrow.

The Creative Power of Thought

THE POWER of thought is the creative power of all life. As you think, so you become; and so you create the conditions that surround you. You must learn to use your good thought. Within you all is this divine creative principle, which has the power to create vibration among, and to control, the actual atoms of matter. We tell you this to help you, for all have the divine urge to know and to become aware of a life which is free, which is holy, happy, healthy and joyous, a life in which you can render service to the world and in which you can see quite clearly the Land of Light. If you would have a better world, create it for yourselves now at this very instant in your mind: hold the thought there continually. Refuse to allow any other thought to banish it from your consciousness, and then raise your whole vibrations and your aspirations. It does no good to dwell on darkness.

So many of our friends among you make the mistake of descending to the level of conflict in their minds. They think of the worst, they see the worst; they allow themselves to be drawn into conversation about the worst that might happen. Remember that every negative thought goes out into the universe and adds to the sum of negative thought in the whole of life. Remember also, however, that the same applies to good thought. A brother–sister of the light dwells in the spirit, sees good, and knows that all works together for good. If you train yourselves to think positively of good, to see good and believe in good, you are serving the whole of creation. You are raising the life-consciousness of all creation. Your little contribution to the whole is of enormous importance.

Never allow yourselves to dwell in darkness or fear or inharmony. If you will transfer your thoughts from physical matter to spiritual life, you will solve your problems. This is a truth, even if it is one you cannot appreciate at present. Nevertheless, practise what we say. Do not think about physical conditions or problems of the earth. Think about God and you will be with God; you will be in God's kingdom. Do not allow your thoughts to limit your life, or the life-force which continually flows into you. You limit this power by negative thoughts, but its flow increases in you and in your life when you attune your thoughts to the Star.

Thought is a living thing, and it can be increased in effectiveness by the power of prayer, and faith, and hard work. You do not sit down and say, 'Dear God, provide for me'. You say, 'I have a pair of hands, here am I. Lead me to my work, wherever it may lie'. You set in motion a thought, and if it is a good thought it attracts the spiritual atoms. It goes on working, not only physically, but in people's hearts and souls. *Nothing in your life is so important as your God-thought.* Your best work, both for your own happiness and health and for your service to humankind, will be done if you will close all the doors of your 'lodge'—by which we mean the holy space you create within and around you. Do not allow the negative thoughts and destructive vibrations of the outer world to penetrate it. You may think this selfish and self-centred, but it is not so. It is the reverse, for it means that you are becoming strong within; you are learning to become a master—master of your own body, master of your own lodge. It also means that you can give far greater healing and light and strength to the suffering people in the world, to help them overcome their difficulties. Instead of your being sucked down into chaos and darkness, you are becoming strong to help.

Your mortal mind will have many arguments against our words. We know; oh, we understand, but we remind you that you have a divine mind as well as a mind of earth! Bring this mind into action. See the perfect life, the life that *we* know in the world of spirit: a life wherein all have learnt to work together for the good of the whole. This is the creative goodness that you can project into your world. Look up to the light and become great channels for the light, and refuse to listen to the mind when it tempts you to give way to despondency. Keep the light burning steadily in your heart.

You can still the storm, you can become serene and still. You can bring forth the higher life in your own being. In your daily life you can attain tranquillity of mind instantly. It is difficult, we know, but to be able to do it you must keep on practising. Every day, before you start your daily work, practise centring yourself, even if only for five minutes. Stop your outer activity. Send your thoughts to those in spirit who are watching and helping you. Let this spiritual life become a living thing, so that it is always with you.

Practise the presence of God, even if only for five minutes in the morning and a few minutes before sleep. Relax mind and body and quietly and slowly breathe deeply. As you breathe in, try to imagine that you are breathing in light and life; that you are not only inhaling air, you are filling every particle of your being with light. As you do this, you will forget your body, and you will be freed from earthly problems. You will, if only for a fleeting moment, be released from the bondage of care and limitation. As this love fills your heart and your mind, every atom, every cell of your body will be filled with perfect life.

The Power of Love to bring Happiness

The power of love brings deep happiness, unfading beauty into a life. The power of love overcomes all obstacles and indeed all darkness, since no darkness remains when love grows strong in the human heart. Learn to give from your heart the perfect love. Even in the spirit world, your promised land—your heaven— can only come to you through what is in your own heart. Do not be carried away by earthly intellect; the mind is so powerful that you can safely allow the heart full play, and you cannot go far wrong if you let your heart guide you always. Work constantly to bring about a blending of the mind and the heart. Act to and from the heart. Do not be content with words; get to the inner meaning of life, to the heart of a brother, a sister, to the heart of a group, to the heart of humanity, and the heart of the earth. Attune yourself to the one keynote of life—love.

Be happy; be full of joy and thankfulness. Within you is the golden light of the Sun, and only you can release this radiation from within your own centre.

Try to realize that your heart centre is the same golden, blazing sun as the one you contemplate in your aspirations. We would have you connect the two—the sun without and the sun within your being. Try to realize, to make real, this infinite source of power that is within you. You can generate a power in yourself that, like the winds of heaven, will sweep clean your surroundings so that all mists will disappear. The conditions of your life will change. More important than this, you yourself will change so that the things of earth that have in the past seemed so tiresome will no longer have any effect. You will regard them in the right perspective, seeing that they are unimportant. You are a child of God, and God has planted within you power to be happy, to overcome all darkness, all sickness, and to enter into perfect life.

On a sunny morning when the birds are singing and the soft winds are blowing through the trees and flowers, you may say, 'Oh, it is good to be alive!'. God's sunshine is bringing this inspiration. But the spiritual sunshine is always there, no matter if the day is dark. The sun is shining, though it may be obscured by mists. Earthly people live with a barrier all around them, which is like a dense fog. The only things that will disperse this fog are spiritual sunlight and the winds of heaven. A light burns within you; you are the only person who can uncover that light and cause it to shine brightly so that the fogs of earth are dispersed. The windows of the soul must be flung wide, every day, to let in the sunlight. We know that sometimes the windows are barred and the latch stiff, and it is difficult to throw open the casement, but it must be done so that sunlight can pour into the soul.

Present yourself each morning before your day's work to the Divine Presence, and your day will be peaceful and happy. See yourself as you truly are, a son or a daughter of the blazing, golden light of the Sun. Seek the light, my child; rise from the earth, and turn your face to the Sun, breathing in the breath of life. Within you is the power of God.

A Power for Peace

You seek, you hope, you pray for peace on earth. Before you can hope for peace on earth you must know peace within your own heart. We work for this: for the peace of the spirit in every human being. Train yourselves in the way of serenity, tranquillity, inward peace. Find that inner tranquillity, and then you will be a power for peace.

You are continually sending out thoughts for world peace. This is not enough now. We ask you to do more than this. We ask you to act peacefully in your individual lives. To put it very simply, if another attacks you do not retaliate, but bring peace to bear upon your brother or sister. If the action of another irritates you and you chafe under a sense of injustice, do not try to attack, even in your thoughts, the one who appears to have offended. There is only one way for you to act: give peace, and give love.

To you all, a last word for now: *do not fear the future*. Do not fear the unknown, not even death itself. For with every forward step you take you are entering a fuller existence. Even if you lose your present body, this only enables you to step forward into a world of light. Here on your earth, by your thoughts, by your aspirations and your actions you are preparing yourself to awaken in a new world. As you step forward you will carry the light, which will reveal the wonders awaiting you. And all the beauties of the spirit life that will be revealed to you emanate from your own soul.

Within, my brethren, within is the Light; give it forth.

CHAPTER SIX

THE WAY OF SERENITY

---

*Concentrate upon the inner light—on tranquillity,
on joy of the spirit—and you have everything. If
you live tranquilly and patiently, always with the
consciousness of God's love upholding you, you will
find that all your life will be heaven.*

Raise your Consciousness to the Light

KEEP the light burning steadily in your heart.
We say this to you, my children, because we
know it is the thing that can help you in your
human life. You find many distractions for the mind,
many disturbances of the emotions. Always remind
yourselves that within you is the Light, the Almighty
Presence, which has all power: power over your mind
and emotions, power over your physical body and
material life. We have learnt from experience that the
way to attain this tranquillity of spirit is to surrender

life and all its emotions, to surrender all anxiety and fear and irritations, to the Light.

If your heart is sore, if you are lonely, anxious, sick or troubled, try to attune yourself and to have confidence in the Source of your being, the Great Light. You will then have no need to seek an answer to your problem. You won't bother about what is going to happen to you in the future, because you will know that all is good. Train yourself to live in the unwavering consciousness that with God—good, love—all things are possible. God is within your innermost being, and if only you will train yourselves to realize this, that you are the point within the circle, God—that you are the point within the blazing Star— you will find peace, deep peace in your heart. You will be still, at rest; you will know divine love. All your thoughts and speech and action will be spontaneously directed from the heart of divine love. It is light, it is the sun, the Sun–Star of God within you.

The Star, which is based on divine love, is the creator of the perfect life, and all humanity will in time achieve the object, the goal of their life, which is to be fully conscious of life within this blazing Star. One day each person will recognize that shining Presence within him- or herself, and will become that blazing Star.

We beg you to remember that the symbol of the Star is the most powerful in your life; it is the most beautiful. You have been given this symbol and this knowledge to use for the glory of God, and the radiation of the light of healing for all the ills of humanity, and for the drawing together of all souls into one family. All the created life of God is drawn together through the love of God manifesting in human life. All are one in the Christ Star.

Your Training in Steadfast Thought

Keep in your hearts, like a shining jewel, the presence of God, and share this presence with those about you. Each hour, each day, each week that you maintain your inner poise and strength of purpose, in good time brings release. As soon as you can make that contact, my brethren, all the little worries of the physical life will miraculously fall into place, and the pattern will become perfect.

You must learn to step outside your personality, or your self as a limited and confining thing; you will learn to get away from yourself, and from the limitations of your physical brain, and to slip away from them on the wings of imagery. You will find yourself free. In this land of meditation, which is no less than the real land of light, you will see behind the scenes of physical and material life, and in doing so learn the true meaning of brotherhood. You must and will learn that you are spirit, that you live and have your being in the Great White Spirit, and that behind you is this power, this life-force, which is your strength, your guide, your help.

Remember always that you do not walk the path of earth life alone, for always your teacher in spirit is by your side, and will never fail you. When you pray for understanding, it will come to you; but it will come to you first in your heart-mind, not in the mind of earth. This is why we try to bring home to you all the realization of the light of God, the light which is called the Christ, in all humanity, the light in your heart. If you are true to the inner light and give your confidence to God, trusting your heavenly Father–Mother and the messengers of the Great Spirit, you can be quite sure that as you tread your path you will be helped in countless ways.

The Truth Within

There is no hurry, remember: no hurry in the spiritual sense. When you are in doubt, be still and wait. When doubt no longer exists for you, then go forward with courage.

So long as mists of doubt envelop you, wait; be still. Be still until the sunlight pours through and dispels the mists ... as it surely will. Or when you are in the shadows, or feel that the shadows are near, remember to look up, to visualize the blazing Sun above you in the spirit spheres, and to feel its strength, its steadiness, pouring into your heart. Go forward in confidence and in full consciousness of the light of this Sun shining upon you.

Always be guided and directed by spiritual principles and laws; let spiritual law rule your daily life and you will do very well. The true craftsperson makes use of the working tools of his or her craft. In other words he or she applies spiritual principles to daily life. When you too can do this you will find inner peace and surety, because you will have set in motion forces that will work constructively in your life and in your world. This is the meaning of brotherhood. Brotherhood is love, service and peace of heart.

We understand how difficult it is for you, moving in the everyday world, to retain inner tranquillity. You speak of peace, you pray for peace, you seek peace on earth. The way to realize this ideal is for you consciously to live in tranquillity. This is not easy to attain, particularly in the busy city and harassed by the constant disturbance and irritation of the massed thought of humankind. There is only one way, and this is to withdraw from the daily conflict for short periods, *but constantly*. You need to withdraw daily from the turmoil of your outer existence, and seek the place of silence within your own being. Here the little spark of spirit within your own being will be reached. Be responsive to that infinite and eternal power. When you are fearful, downcast, hesitant, turn to that still centre within and rest there. All will be well.

61

This experience cannot come by reading books, or studying the history of nations, or studying the religions of all time. It can only come to you as you endeavour to find the silent power—that gentle, pure love deep within your heart. Some rush about the world trying to contact some sacred centre, or to meet some 'holy man' with whom to talk. All the while, if they will only turn within, turn to that silent centre within, all the holy men of past and present will draw close to them in their own sanctuary, in their own home. The light and power and companionship of the holy ones of all time will be with them instantly.

If you would be happy and give happiness to all whom you contact, seek the quiet places of the spirit, and discriminate between the unreal, which is of the world, and the reality, which is of the spirit. We would guide you to seek truth—not by reading books, but by going into the silence, creating in your higher mind the most beautiful forms of nature. Go into the eternal and infinite garden in meditation, and you will learn so much. Don't let that earthly mind get entangled with the mind in your soul, the higher mind, and pull you down. First be still ... cultivate that attitude of mind which recognizes the difference between the outer personality, the outer self, and the inner; and remember that your thoughts and emotions and all the activities of your mental vehicles all belong to the outer self.

The real place of stillness is deep within.... It is like

an unruffled lake, and when you stand by that lake and gaze into the still waters you will see ... yourself. Just be still and meditate beside the still waters, absorbing the peace and stillness. You will no longer be swayed by the voices of men and women, or the mental and emotional winds which blow hither and thither; you will develop that poise and strength in yourself which will give you a clear perception of truth and help you to put first things first in your life. And the first things are the things of the spirit.

Give yourselves times every day to relax your physical activity, completely to relax, and attune your consciousness to the enfolding and inflowing light and love of the Great White Spirit. *You can do as much for the whole world as vast armies*. Shall we put it that way?

It is through the individual awareness of the great Love permeating all creation and all humankind that the world will come to the new golden age. Every man and woman, no matter how low they have sunk or how evil they may appear to be, have within them the need for love and the desire to love. Love is the solvent; love will cure the world of all its ills.

Do not forget to turn to that inner light for your succour and guidance. In the inner light you may meet the brethren who work behind the scenes of the material life to send forth the light of the Star to suffering humanity. They—the Brethren—never doubt, they never look on the dark side; they live in the Light and work with the Light. They *are* the Light. We ask you to follow their example and teaching. The secret of strength lies in the quiet mind.

Our World can be Yours

We want you now to draw away from the world of earth and all its noise and babble, and to enter into *our* world, the inner world, where peace, beauty and love are centred. These are the qualities you will find when you learn to step inside the temple of the spirit, the temple of God ... the white temple on the hill, if you prefer. We ask you most earnestly to strive to do this, because in this way you will help all humankind. So many think that to pray and meditate is a waste of time when so much practical work is waiting to be done. Practical work can go very wrong if it is not guided by the stillness and truth of the Christ spirit. Therefore we say, be still.... Come into this pure white temple and there hold communion with the holiness and the purity of your Creator, the infinite and eternal heavenly Father and Mother. Do not strive too hard or force meditation; rather let it *be* in you, so that at any time or in any place you can turn inwards, and by practice and self-training, reach the inner temple of your heart, silent, empty, still ... and wait.

Here you will feel only love—a perfect calm and

an all-embracing love that will also flow out from you as waves of love into the universal. So you will become conscious of the embrace of the infinite and the universal, and in that love you will realize that none can be your enemy. No-one of themselves has the power to raise you to heights or cast you into the depths. You can feel only love, at-one-ment, and a perfect brotherhood with all humankind and all creation.

We bless you, and we say once again that the answer to your own individual problem and heartache is to surrender ... surrender all to God ... to be still within.

Be calm. Do not press and overwork yourself.

Be calm, do your work quietly, do not try to overdrive your life. Live as the flowers live, opening your hearts to the warmth and radiance of the Sun.

In Silence shall be your Strength

It is not so much what is happening round you that is important. It is the way you deal with the happenings. Learn to be calm, to be still, to do your best. Learn to live so as to express the love that has been planted in your heart. You will never again be torn by emotion, nor will you be puzzled; because there, within yourself, you will find the still, ever-burning flame—so bright, so bright, a flame of the spiritual sun. As you concentrate on that pure, bright, white flame, you will feel the majesty of the sun in yourself: you will know that you are master of your body, of the conditions of your life. Nothing can touch you.

When you go out into the world, do not forget those silent moments when, within the quiet of your inmost sanctuary, you have been aware of a spiritual power, of the touch of angels' wings. In the stress of the world, keep the sweetness of the Christ spirit ever with you. In silence shall be your strength. If you will withdraw from the outer confusion and conflict of human life into the inner peace of your agelong spirit, you will become strong. You can get worked up and indeed make yourselves ill; or you can keep very still and continuously seek the place of silence and strength. You can examine your problem and you can say, 'I would have the strength to handle this situation as the Master would handle it.'*

The Master would warn you against allowing yourself to be caught up in the vortex of physical and material problems. At least withdraw from them at stated times in the day. There are times to work, times to rest. You feel you have too much to do—but, you know, it is not the amount of work, it is the way you do it that causes you to be battered and worn out. It is your attitude of mind towards that work.

*A favourite phrase from White Eagle's teaching, and one used in his books HEAL THYSELF and PRAYER, MINDFULNESS AND INNER CHANGE.

Remember every morning as you wake, and every evening before you go to rest, that you are held within the love of your heavenly Father and Mother, and you will be uplifted and relieved of all tension. Open your heart to the inflow of that great Sun-life, until your whole being, body and soul and spirit, becomes charged again and again with divine Life. When you are in doubt, confusion, fear, seek your own inner sanctuary, the sanctuary of your heart.

Visualize your surroundings in the spirit sphere of life, in a small white and gold chapel. Train yourself in the entering of your own white chapel, until it becomes even more real to you than any physical form to which you are accustomed. Go within, into the heavenly silence. Seek there the inner silence, the stillness of the pure spirit. In this shall your strength lie.

When you look on human suffering, while you give sympathy, kindness and understanding, do not be dragged down by it. Do not allow your emotions to sweep you along like a piece of straw on the winds. Be still in your sanctuary and look into the heart of the blazing Star. From the centre of this Star the light flows into your heart and your whole being. Let it be like a strong sword to you, a sword of the spirit that will withstand all negative conditions. There is so much confusion of thought, so much turmoil all round you in the world that you need help to give you more confidence and strength of purpose. When you rise beyond the lower level into the light of the

67

Christ life, you are no longer confused but filled with knowledge. Your way is certain, your body is healed.

CHAPTER SEVEN

ASPIRING TO HAPPINESS

As the light and love of God within your life increase, so that which formerly hurt you has no more power. Be free, and happy in the life God has given you. Then you are well on the road to heavenly happiness and regeneration.

Cast out Fear

DO YOU need to be asked to have faith? No! You are children of the Light! So cast out fear. When we come down through the mists of the astral into the greater mists of the earth, we feel and see the suffering caused through fear, and we see that the basis of most suffering is fear. We see the human mind filled with fear of the unknown, fear of the future. We notice how easy it is for you to get into a state of fear and doubt. When you find yourself fearing either for yourself, your health, your conditions, the world, or anything which comes into your life, you are weakening yourself. Let go. We tell you this again: place your whole confidence in God, at the very moment fear arises.

Take your thoughts to your higher, spiritual self, which knows that fear is unnecessary. Nothing happens by chance. If you live tranquilly, patiently, always with this consciousness of God's love behind you and through you, you will find that whatever has crept in and seemingly spoilt your life will gradually be resolved. If you just take your hands off and keep quiet, be still and let God work His–Her Will, all will be perfectly harmonious, all will be peaceful and will work together. Greater work is being done on your earth than you know with your earthly mind. There is a mighty increase of spiritual power and an awakening of the Christ Light in the hearts of many, many people.

We ask you to create in your mind the image of a perfect world, a perfect land. The way for you to restore the true way of life on this planet, to restore harmony and brotherhood, is to hold humanity and indeed the earth itself in a perfect thought, a thought of harmony, of brotherly love and wholeness, or healthiness. If a person of peace enters a noisy room where others are speaking in loud voices and indulging in argument and dissension, with a very few words he or she can restore peace and quietude in the company. This, my brethren, you need to do today on earth. Do not add fuel to fire by discussing wars and future wars; do not look into the future with fear, and have no part in conversation about fear and destruction. See the nations being drawn together in federation, in brotherhood. Know that this is to be, because this is the Divine Will. In spiritual law there can be no compromise and no excuse; law is law, and spiritual law is the law of brotherhood and love and tranquillity. See the nations walking together as brothers in the sunlight. This is the way to restore the peace on earth.

The Star is the Key

A long time has passed, my children, since you left that heavenly home, that world of sunlight, the spiritual Sun from which you all originated; and so you forget that you are spirit, born of God, and eternally linked with God. You have to learn consciously to remember that you are a part of this eternal spiritual Sun. Light will shine on your life and your fears will dissolve. You will discover later on that your cloud has a silver lining, and you will find completion, happiness, service. If you have to cross a bridge, you will have a very wise and strong companion by your side, holding your hand, crossing the bridge with you. In time you will find great power welling up within.

Put your hand out to God; He–She will clasp your hand and draw you up. God is within your innermost being, and if you will train yourselves to realize this— that you are the point within the circle, God—that you are the point within the blazing Star, then you will find peace, deep peace, in your heart. You will be still, at rest; you will know divine love; all your thoughts and speech and action will be spontaneously directed from the heart of divine love. Live in the unwavering consciousness that with God—good, love—all things are possible. God holds the power for you, and every experience is to bring you right into the heart of God's love. This is your goal, and the happenings on earth are all stepping-stones leading you to your goal.

God holds the key. It is light; it is the Star of God within you. The Star, which is based on divine love, is the creator of the perfect life, and all humanity will in time achieve the object, the goal of their life, which is to be fully conscious of life within this blazing Star. Remember the shining Star Brotherhood, that great multitude in the heavens, the Brotherhood of the Light. They know no darkness, doubt or fear. They know that all is moving forward to ultimate brotherhood. All the good, the true and the beautiful things on your earth are inspired and guided and brought into manifestation by the true Brotherhood: the Brotherhood of the Star. Try to expand in consciousness and realize the immensity of that great Star Brotherhood. You live confined in your physical bodies, which are like little closed boxes; but if you will, by aspiration and inspiration, strive to reach that vast Brotherhood, you will receive the greatest good. Try to become *en rapport* with that ancient and limitless Brotherhood of Life. One day every person will recognize that shining Presence within him or her, and will become that blazing Star.

Keep your vision on the Star, brethren. A flood of heavenly light is poured upon you, now. May you be caught up in this glory of the Eternal Light, the very Life of God.

The Angel by your Side

Never forget the angel by your side. Hold the hand of love and true humility in your work. Leave the thoughts of the earth and rise in spirit to the spheres of light. We take you up into the world of light, your real home, the home of the spirit and the soul, and we move amongst our brethren in the heavenly garden. You meditate on the world of nature, but remember also heavenly nature, for all growing things on earth receive the life forces from the heaven world. We work with you to stimulate your awareness of this infinite and eternal life, the beauty of the life of God.

Come with us into the heavenly garden and walk with the Brethren of the Light. Talk with your own teacher and guide, commune with the angelic company.

In the infinite and eternal garden you will see angelic forces still and peaceful, continually giving, giving help, pouring love and wisdom upon creation.

This is the truth we wish to bring home to all our brothers, this harmonious working between God and humanity. You are called to do certain work, it is true, but do remember that whatever your work is, you are making a spiritual contribution. So fill your hearts with love and compassion, and keep in tune at all times with the invisible host. The love which you will feel as you do this is not just a surface emotion, it is a real love which comes from God, from the heart; and as you feel that love, you will be able to open your heart ever wider to receive that golden Sunlight from the heart of God; it will shine into your heart to strengthen you, to give you vision and understanding. Understand that all power is given to the soul who loves God, the power of love to understand. We tell you again that it can illumine a room when the soul possessing such a love enters that room. The power of love uplifts, and points the way to God.

The Gift of Happiness

You listen to our words because your soul aspires to that which lies beyond material life. You search for truth and, more, you search for happiness—for you, for yours.

What do we mean by happiness? Does this imply that we shall each get all our material desires and longings satisfied? Will this form of satisfaction bring us lasting happiness? You will not find this method will produce the desired result. What then makes for true happiness? Before you can answer you must ask yourself whether you have ever experienced true happiness, apart from the pleasure of the moment— for happiness can come sometimes in the midst of great sorrow.

Happiness, my friends, is realization of God in the heart. Happiness is won as the result of praise, of thanksgiving, of faith and of acceptance of God. All these bring to the spirit a perfect and indescribable joy and serenity—a quiet, tranquil realization of the Light of God arising from true discernment, true discrimination and true faith. For God is happiness.

And so, my friends, we do not wish you good luck; we do not wish you prosperity; we do not even wish you good health ... we would rather wish you the supreme happiness resulting from the union of your spirit with the Great White Light, with Christ, and all his angels. We wish you the heavenly happiness which no earthly event can ever steal away

May you find such happiness as this in days to come; and may you shed light in the pathway of others and thus share your happiness with all those near and dear to you, and with humanity. Amen.

A MEDITATION

BRETHREN, close your eyes, close your senses to the outer world. Imagine that we are all sitting around a camp fire under a starlit sky with the brotherhood of nature. We are watching the camp fire burning in our midst, smelling the perfumes of the earth, the pines and the flowers and woods; we are looking up to the canopy of heaven, gazing upon the stars' twinkling light. The stars mean more to us than just lights in the sky—they mean those powers of God which can destroy and create.

We learn to accept all that God sends to us as being good, for we understand that the Great White Spirit is in supreme command; we know that the stars and planets and the great planetary beings and angels, right down to our little nature spirits, obey the command. The brethren are gathered in the hush of the evening, listening to the orchestra of nature. They hear the wind in the pines and the murmur of the insects, the faint twitter of birds, the sound of furry beasts, beaver and rat and all the tiny creatures of water and woods. All are one great happy brotherhood living under the protection and by the love of the invisible power, the Great White Spirit. Even as we turn our gaze to the stars, the stars speak to our innermost heart of love, of brotherhood, of peace....

*

Why do we tell you to do this tonight? We are endeavouring to bring each one of you awareness of the vast brotherhood of life.

Live and rest in this consciousness. This is what you have to live for, my dear ones; do not rush and tear about and get anxious and worried over things which do not matter. The creatures of God are all your brethren. Be at peace, radiate peace.... Quietly perform your tasks, keeping always within your heart the memory of life, true life, the life which is yours always and which you share with God and all his creatures.

And now may the peace of the eternal stillness, the tranquillity of spirit, abide with you, in all your ways. *Good night, beloved. Be kind, be gentle, be at peace.*

NOTES

The quotation 'not a sparrow shall fall on the ground' on p. 16 is a slight rephrasing of St Matthew 10 : 29. On page 35, the phrase about a peace that the world can neither give nor take away comes from the Prayer Book. Page 38 includes a reference to the Twenty-third Psalm: 'lead you into green pastures and beside still waters'.

In the final meditation, White Eagle speaks of telling his hearers to listen. He says, 'why do we tell you to do this tonight?'. Somehow, even though 'tonight' may puzzle the reader of this book, the word seems to bring some of the atmosphere of the talk at which the meditation was first given—or even of the campfire seen that White Eagle is trying to reproduce for us.

THE WHITE EAGLE PUBLISHING TRUST, which publishes and distributes the White Eagle teaching, is part of the wider work of the White Eagle Lodge, a present-day school of wisdom in which people may find a place for growth and understanding, and a place in which the teachings of White Eagle find practical expression. Here men and women may come to learn the reason for their life on earth and how to serve and live in harmony with the whole brotherhood of life, visible and invisible, in health and happiness.

The White Eagle Publishing Trust website is at www.whiteaglepublishing.org.

Readers wishing to know more of the work of the White Eagle Lodge may write to The White Eagle Lodge, New Lands, Brewells Lane, Liss, Hampshire, England GU33 7HY (tel. 01730 893300) or can call at The White Eagle Lodge, 9 St Mary Abbots Place, Kensington, London W8 6LS (tel. 020-7603 7914). In the Americas please write to The Church of the White Eagle Lodge at P. O. Box 930, Montgomery, Texas 77356 (tel. 936-597 5757), and in Australasia to The White Eagle Lodge (Australasia), P. O. Box 225, Maleny, Queensland 4552, Australia (tel. 07-5494 4397).

Our websites and email addresses are as follows.
www.whiteagle.org; enquiries@whiteagle.org (worldwide);
www.whiteaglelodge.org; sjrc@whiteaglelodge.org (Americas);
www.whiteagle.ca (Canada); and www.whiteeaglelodge.org.au;
enquiries@whiteeaglelodge.org.au (Australasia)